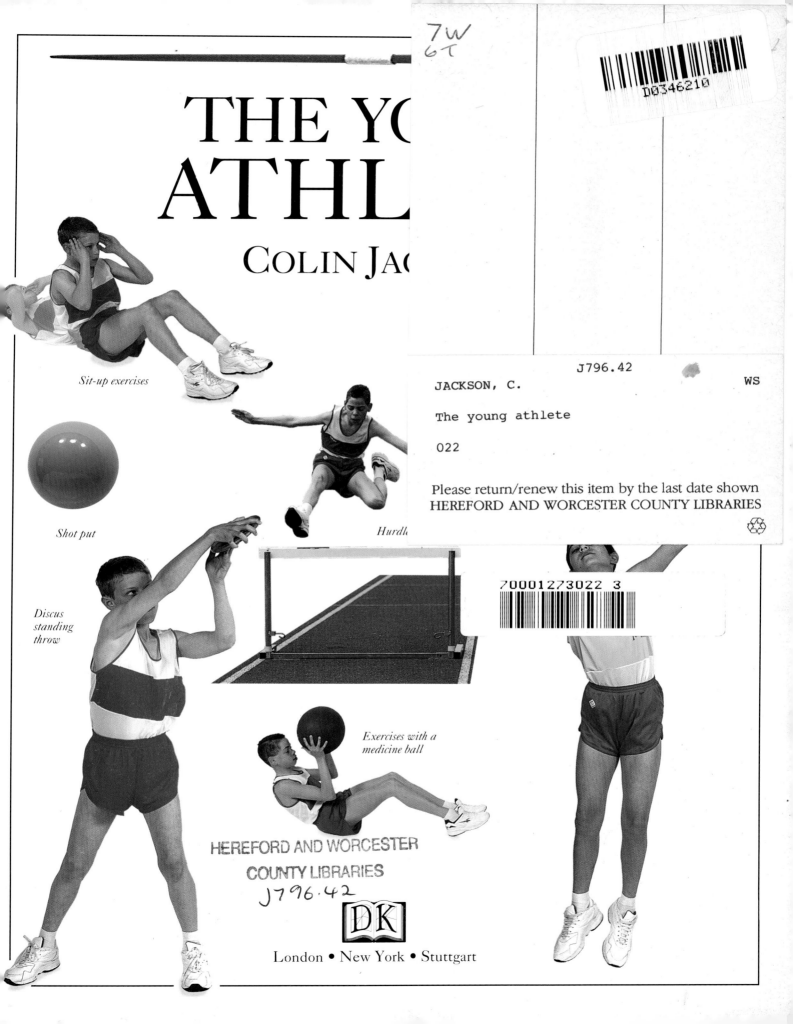

THE YOUNG ATHLETE

COLIN JACKSON

Sit-up exercises

Shot put

Hurdl

Discus standing throw

Exercises with a medicine ball

DK

London • New York • Stuttgart

A DORLING KINDERSLEY BOOK

Project editor Fiona Robertson   **Art editor** Rebecca Johns

Photography John Garrett

Picture research Sharon Southren

Production Charlotte Traill

Deputy editorial director Sophie Mitchell

Deputy art director Miranda Kennedy

The young athletes
Nathan Allen, Sholeh Anghaee,
Josselyne Engele, James Maudner, John Reid,
Ruth Tchaparian

First published in Great Britain in 1996 by
Dorling Kindersley Limited
9 Henrietta Street, London WC2E 8PS

A CIP catalogue record for this book is available from the British Library.

ISBN 0 7513 5370 1

Colour reproduction by Colourscan, Singapore
Printed by Graphicom in Italy

Contents

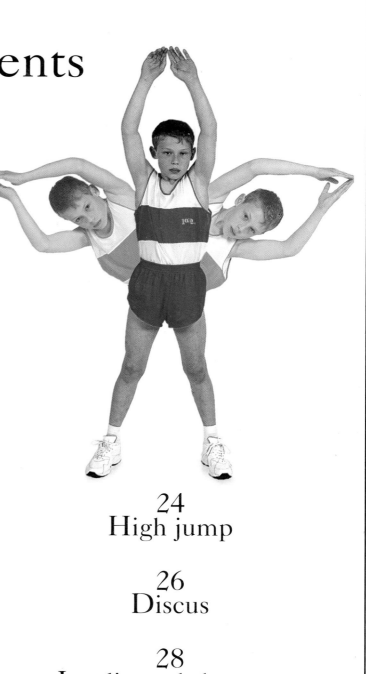

To all young athletes

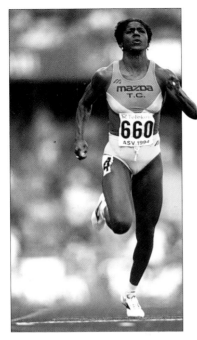

"It takes lots of self-discipline, commitment, and energy to be a successful athlete."

"**A**THLETICS IS A GREAT COMPETITIVE sport which continues to give me constant enjoyment. I took part in many different sports at school, and considered being a decathlete before concentrating on hurdling when I was 17 years old. The hurdles are the most technical of all the athletic events and the barriers provide a daunting challenge in an event that covers 110 metres and lasts under 13 seconds. The training is hard and punishing, but winning gold at the World Championships makes it all worthwhile. I have been one of the lucky ones to reach the top in athletics, but at any level the main thing is to enjoy the many events that athletics can offer. I hope you enjoy reading this book and have as much fun with your athletics as I do – best of luck!"

"Athletics is rarely considered a team sport, but during the relay, we all work together to get the baton around the track as quickly as possible."

At the World Championships
Colin Jackson with the gold medal he won for the 110 m hurdles at the 1993 World Championships in Stuttgart. His time of 12.91 seconds set a new World Record.

"Once you are in a race, you realize that all the hard training is worthwhile."

"You have to give each race everything you've got!"

"Athletics is great fun and has a tendency to keep you young in your outlook."

History of athletics

ATHLETICS IS THE OLDEST FORM of organized sport. It is actually a collection of different sports and dates back to ancient times, when running, jumping, and throwing events were seen as vital training for hunting and warfare. The first Olympic Games were held in 776 BC at Olympia in Greece. The Games were held every four years in honour of the god Zeus and many of the events in the modern Games have their roots in these ancient beginnings.

Ancient Games, Olympia
Runners in the original Olympic Games at Olympia in Ancient Greece, above, wore helmets and carried shields, but competed naked. At the first recorded Games, in 776 BC, there was only one event, the stade race. The number of events and the length of the Games gradually increased until they were abolished altogether in 393 AD.

First Olympic Committee
The first meeting of the International Olympic Committee (IOC), in 1896, is shown above. Seated on the left is the Frenchman, Baron Pierre de Coubertin, who founded the modern Olympics. Also present are representatives from Greece, Germany, the former Soviet Union, Czechoslovakia, Hungary, and Sweden.

Athens, 1896
One of the first competitions in the 1896 Olympics was the 100 m, above. It was won by Thomas Burke of the US who completed it in 12.0 seconds. Burke is second from left in the picture.

World record beater
Jesse Owens, above, set a remarkable record in the 1936 games in Berlin, Germany, by winning four gold medals within an hour for the 100 m, the 200 m, the long jump, and as a member of the 4 x 100 m relay team.

The opening ceremony
The Olympics are opened by a member of the host country's Royal Family or national government. At the opening ceremony, the Olympic flame is brought into the stadium by a team of relay runners who have carried it from Olympia in Greece. The 1992 ceremony in Barcelona, Spain, is shown left.

An athletics stadium
A stadium is arranged so that both running (or track) and jumping and throwing (or field) events can take place at the same time. The modern track is oval-shaped, measures 400 m around, and has between six and ten lanes. The track surface is usually made of plastic or rubber, which makes it both weather-resistant and hard-wearing. The field events take place in the centre of the track. This area is called the infield.

200 m
3000 m and 5000 m
Back straight
3000 m steeplechase
Pole vault
1500 m
Javelin
Shot put
110 m hurdles
100 m 100 m hurdles
Long jump
Home straight
Triple jump
Finish line for all events
10,000 m
High jump
Relays, 400 m, 400 m hurdles
800 m

Starting athletics

WHEN YOU FIRST START athletics, you will need some comfortable clothes that allow you plenty of movement. Choose lightweight materials that are absorbent and easy to wash. The most important item of your kit is your training shoes. If you decide to continue in athletics, you will eventually need specialized shoes for the different events. However, to begin with, a pair of general purpose, or "cross", training shoes will do. Make sure there is a layer of cushioning the length of the shoe to absorb the impact of running and jumping.

Boys' kit

For training, most boys wear a singlet which is tucked into shorts. The shorts should be loose enough to allow your legs to move freely. Most athletes have more than one singlet; a club one for competitions and at least one or two others for training. You can carry all these items in a sports bag.

Training shoes

Your training shoes should be both comfortable and supportive. Running or cross training shoes can be used for most athletic events. They do not have to be expensive, but they must be a good fit. Never buy shoes that are a size too big; you will find them difficult to run in and the slippage may cause painful blisters or a sprained ankle.

Make sure the tread on your soles is not worn.

Layer of cushioning

Note the wider shoulder strap on the girl's singlet.

Choose a sports bag that has shoulder straps as well as handles.

Holes in the singlet allow air to circulate.

Cotton is still the best material for the singlet because it absorbs sweat.

Cotton ankle socks absorb sweat from your feet.

Always tie your laces properly, in a double knot if necessary.

Girls' kit

The girls' kit is very similar to the boys'. However, the girl's singlet is wider at the shoulder and higher both at the front and under the arms. Many girls now also wear leotards, which range from being high cut to knee length.

Tracksuit

Tracksuits are an important part of your kit, both in cold and warm weather. Whether you are training or competing, a lot of your time will be spent recovering and your muscles must be kept warm to avoid strains and injuries. Tracksuits come in various materials from waterproof to light cotton. Make sure that the one you get is comfortable.

Some tracksuit tops have collars that can be rolled up or down when zipped up. These are ideal in cold weather.

Long hair should be tied back.

Make sure your tracksuit doesn't restrict your movements.

Your tracksuit may have your team's logo on it.

Buy a tracksuit with zipped pockets to protect against losing items.

An ankle zip allows you to remove your tracksuit bottoms over your shoes quickly.

Joining a club

Before joining a club, you should visit the track and talk to other athletes and club officials to find out what is on offer. Ensure that there are coaches to give you training and that there will be club competitions for your age group. Some clubs provide a free singlet or free track use with their membership.

The minimum equipment that you need to join a club is a club singlet, shorts, and training shoes.

Many club singlets have their club logo on them and that of their team's sponsor. There are often restrictions on the size of the lettering.

Clubs have registered colours for their singlet and shorts.

Club singlets must be worn in competitions.

Fasten your competition number to your singlet with safety pins.

Numbers

Competitors wear numbers on their chest and back so that they can be identified. High jumpers wear just one number on their chest and pole vaulters have one on their backs to avoid getting it caught on the bar.

Most athletes buy shorts that match their singlet.

Spikes

Spikes are used to provide a better grip on the track surface. They are much lighter than training shoes and provide less support. Choose a general pair for training and competing, such as the middle-long distance shoe, which has heel cushioning. Later on you may want a more specialized pair.

Spikes used on rubber tracks should be no more than 6 mm (0.2 in) long.

The spikes in these shoes are removable; always carry a spare set and a spanner in case you lose one.

Warming up

BEFORE YOU TAKE PART in any kind of exercise, you must make sure that your muscles are warm and properly stretched. This keeps you supple and stops you getting injured. Your warm up should last for about 20 minutes. Begin with some gentle jogging to increase your body temperature and then do some stretching exercises. You should also go through a stretching routine after athletics. This allows your body to cool down properly and helps to prevent stiffness the next day.

1 Look over your shoulder. Hold this position for a count of ten.

2 Bring your head back to the centre position and rest.

3 Turn your head to the other side. With each stretch, try to go a bit farther.

Neck exercises

It is a good idea to begin your warm up with neck exercises and work downwards. This will make it easier to remember the sequence of exercises. Make sure you hold your neck in the stretch position during these exercises; never roll it.

1 Tilt your head towards your shoulder. Don't lift your shoulder up to your head.

2 Count to 10, relax, and then do the other side.

3 Lower your chin to touch your chest. Remember to keep your shoulders back.

Arm circling

The muscles in the shoulders are connected to those in the chest. Exercises for one of these areas can therefore also benefit the other area. This exercise loosens the muscles in the arms and shoulders.

Your arms should pass close to your ears at the top of the swing.

Don't let your body move backwards or forwards during this exercise.

Try to breathe normally; don't try to keep pace with the swings.

Keep your arms straight throughout this exercise.

Keep your back straight.

1 Start with your arms by your sides and your feet shoulder-width apart for balance. Keep your arms straight and slowly swing them backwards.

Your legs should be slightly bent.

2 Keep your arms straight as you swing them up past your head and down towards the ground in a big circle.

Bring your arms close to your hips at the bottom of the swing.

3 When your body begins to feel looser, change direction and swing your arms anticlockwise. Never rush the swing; always keep it controlled.

Feet should be shoulder-width apart.

Side bends

The waist, abdomen, and lower back link the actions of the upper and lower body. You must make sure that the muscles in these areas are properly stretched, because you will use them in all athletics.

1 Bend to one side from the hips. Keep your body facing forwards and your hips tilted under. Hold the stretch for 10 seconds; do not bounce.

2 Raise your body back into the upright position and rest for a couple of seconds.

Try to bring your hands together above your head; if you find this too difficult, rest one hand on your thigh instead.

3 Now bend over to the other side, making sure your body is still facing forwards. Keep breathing normally. Next time, try to stretch a little farther.

Keep your body facing forwards during this exercise.

Your legs should be slightly bent.

Feet should be shoulder-width apart.

Hamstring stretch

One of the most common injuries in athletics is a pulled or torn hamstring. This exercise, in which a friend applies gentle pressure to your back, allows you to stretch your hamstring farther than you could on your own.

Press gently so as not to cause strain on the lower back.

With your arms outstretched, relax your body down over your legs and hold your ankles or toes.

Quadriceps stretch

Stretch your quadriceps, or thigh muscle, by pulling back your knee so that your heel touches your bottom. Balance by placing your arm against a wall, a friend's shoulder, or some equipment.

Use this arm for balance.

Don't lock this leg because this will put too much strain on your knee.

Inner thigh stretch

Strains in the inner thigh and the groin area are usually caused by sudden movements. Stretching reduces the chance of this happening by ensuring that the muscle is flexible enough to cope with any changes in length.

Try to keep your shoulders level.

Keep your body upright and facing forwards.

Rest your hands on your legs for balance.

Bend your leg at right angles to your knee with your foot facing forwards.

Controlled movements

Do all the exercises in your warm up slowly, making sure that your movements are smooth and controlled.

Hold your head in line with your body.

To increase the stretch, lower your hips towards the ground slowly.

Keep this leg straight during the stretch, with your foot facing forwards.

Your toes should be in line with your bent knee.

Calf muscle stretch

Stand about 30 cm (12 in) from a wall and lean forwards onto it. Bend your left knee and stretch your right leg backwards. Try to keep your right heel on the ground and feel the stretch in your lower leg.

Keep this heel pressed into the ground.

Push your hips forwards.

Sprint drills

THE SPRINTING EVENTS – the 100 m, the 200 m, and the 400 m – are probably the most popular athletic events. Sprinting requires short, fast explosions of power and the most successful sprinters can combine speed with quick reactions and tremendous stamina. Exercises called sprint drills concentrate on improving these sprinting techniques.

Heel flicks

This drill is designed to make your legs move quicker by improving the speed with which your heel comes up to your bottom. It also strengthens your hamstrings (the muscles running down the back of your leg).

1 Hold your body upright, look straight ahead and start jogging using very short strides.

Loosely cup your hands.

Don't let your knee swing forwards.

2 With each step, pull your heel up sharply so that it makes contact with your bottom.

Pull your elbows back.

Keep your hips high.

Fold this leg up behind you.

High knee lifts

One of the most important techniques in sprinting is the high knee lift. This very powerful movement helps to increase the length of your stride, which in turn makes you go faster. The high knee lift is produced by the hips and the thigh muscles. Events such as throwing the javelin, jumping, and hurdling will also benefit from this drill.

1 Begin by walking or jogging on the balls of your feet. Concentrate on the movements in this drill; think about what the best sprinters look like when they are sprinting towards the finishing line.

2 Bring your knees up to hip height with each stride. Pump your arms backwards and forwards from your hips to your shoulders.

Try to keep your foot flexed during this drill.

Keep your shoulders back; if you lean forwards it's harder to lift your knees.

Relax your jaw and keep your chin up.

Make sure you stay up on the balls of your feet as if you were sprinting.

Look straight ahead.

Practising drills
All of the drills shown here can be done on the spot or while jogging. Each one is practised over a fixed distance or for a fixed number of times.

Ankle rolls

Sprinting is done mostly on the balls of the feet. Ankle rolls help to loosen your ankles and increase their range of movement. This in turn enables you to stay up on the balls of your feet during sprinting. Middle- and long-distance running also benefit from this drill.

Don't tip your head forwards.

Your arm movements can be more relaxed in this drill.

Bring this heel down.

Feet positions

Keep your feet moving along the ground during this drill, but make sure they are never more than a few centimetres apart.

1 Roll right up onto the balls of your feet.

2 Step forwards slightly and bring your heel down.

3 Repeat the drill using your other foot.

3 Repeat the movement using your other leg. Don't let your hips drop during this drill; this is a sign of bad technique.

Keep moving your arms.

Your knee should be at the same height as your hips.

4 High knee lifts can be very tiring at first. Allow yourself a minute or two to recover before you repeat this drill.

Track officials

"On your marks ..... set ..... bang!" As the starter fires his gun, the race begins. The starter has to ensure that all the runners begin at the same time. If any of the runners "false starts" (leaves the starting block before the command), a marksman fires a gun to bring them back to their starting positions. A runner is allowed two false starts before being disqualified from the race. Other race officials include timekeepers and the chief track judge.

Standing start

Middle- and long-distance races use the standing start, which has just one starting command. When you hear "On your marks", place most of your weight on your front foot and lean forwards in a comfortable position, ready to sprint off on the Bang! of the starter's gun. For those who have not yet learned to use the starting blocks (see page 12), this type of start can also be used for the sprinting events.

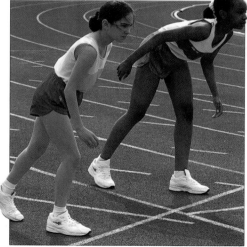

Behind the line

The marksman checks that your feet are behind the line before the race starts.

Starting the race

IN THE EARLY DAYS of athletics, sprinters used to dig small holes in the ground to give them something to push off against at the start of a race. Today, runners in the 100 m, the 200 m, and the 400 m use starting blocks to provide a more solid base to push against. The blocks must be fastened to the track and are fitted with tiny spikes along their edges to ensure they do not damage the track surface.

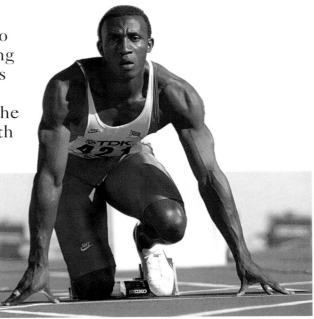

The starting block
A starting block consists of a metal bar with a pair of adjustable foot pads attached to it. The blocks can be connected to a device that detects if a foot has left the block before the starting gun to within 0.1 seconds. This is used to decide if any runner false starts (see page 11).

The foot pads can be moved and their angle adjusted.

Holes for adjusting foot pad.

The hand position
In the "On your marks" position, your hands must be behind the starting line. Use your fingers and thumb to form a bridge; do not lay your palms on the track.

Preparing to run
An athlete's state of mind before a race is as important as his physical condition. Linford Christie, above, is famous for his "tunnel vision" concentration, in which he focuses his mind totally on the race ahead.

On your marks ...

1 When you hear the command "On your marks", position your hands behind the lines and place your feet on the blocks. The front block should be about 30–40 cm (10–12 in) behind the starting line; the other block is the length of your foot behind this.

Be comfortable
You should feel comfortable in the blocks. Experiment until you find the position that suits you best.

2 On "Set", raise your hips and tilt your body forwards so that your shoulders are in line with your arms. Press both feet hard against the blocks ready to drive out.

Your hips should be higher than your shoulders.

To get a good push off the blocks, keep your legs bent.

Your front knee should be in line with your arms.

The rear block should form a right angle with the ground.

If you are not strong enough to take your weight on your fingers, try resting on your knuckles instead.

Running the bend

In the 200 m, the 400 m, and the 4 x 100 m relay, you must stay in your own lane as you run the bend. Because you approach the bend at top speed, you will find that you are pushed to the outside of your lane. To avoid this, take shorter strides and lean into the bend. Try to run close to the inside of your lane as this will reduce the distance you have to run.

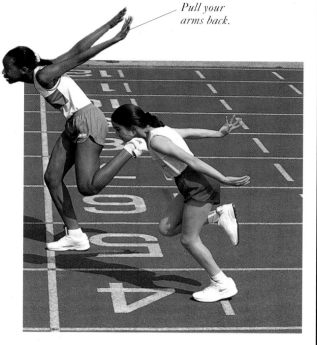

Keep looking ahead; don't look around at the other runners.

Pull your arms back.

Drop your inside arm to help you lean into the bend.

Take shorter strides.

Sprinting to victory

This picture of Frank Fredericks of Namibia was taken at the 1993 World Championships in Stuttgart, Germany. As he approaches the bend on the 200 m, Fredericks's body twists slightly as he drops his left shoulder and leans into the bend. This helps him to keep his legs moving smoothly as he runs the bend. Fredericks won this race.

The finish

A well-timed dip finish can make all the difference to your position in a race. The winner is the person whose torso, or trunk, crosses the finishing line first. About three strides from the line, pull your arms back and thrust your chest and shoulders forwards as you push yourself, or "dip", across the line. Try not to dip too soon however; this will slow you down because you stop pumping your arms.

3 On the "Bang!" of the starter's gun, push back hard against the blocks. Take your hands off the ground as you drive your body forwards.

Leaving the block
Try to run out of the blocks with a smooth, continuous action.

Your hands leave the ground as you push off against the block.

Bring this leg forwards to form your first stride.

Keep your head and body low to improve your acceleration.

Pump your arms backwards and forwards quickly.

Keep looking down at the track; if you raise your head, your hips will drop.

Push your front leg back against the block.

4 As you push hard off the front block, swing your back leg forwards into the first stride. Keep your body low until you reach your top speed and your natural stride length.

Different starts
In the 200 m, the 400 m, and the 800 m, the start is staggered to ensure the athletes run the same distance.

Training for longer distances

THE MAIN MIDDLE- AND LONG-distance events are the 800 m, the 1500 m, the 3000 m, the 5000 m, and the 10,000 m. Runners in these events must be able to run at a steady pace over long distances, and need a slow, constant supply of energy. Training or conditioning programmes help you to build up the stamina and the muscle strength that you need to compete successfully in these races.

Keep your feet apart for balance.

Keep your stomach pulled in.

Don't arch your back.

Try not to lock your arms or dip your body too low.

Press-ups
Support your weight with your hands beneath your shoulders. Keep your body in a straight line and bend your arms to bring your nose down to the ground. If you find a full press-up too difficult, try putting some of your weight on your knees. As you become stronger, gradually move your knees off the ground.

Keep your hands by the side of your head and try not to pull your neck as you curl upwards.

Breathe in as you lower yourself back down.

Breathe out as you come up.

Pull your stomach in as you curl up.

Keep your feet on the ground.

Sit-ups
Strengthen your stomach, or abdominal, muscles by doing sit-ups. Lie on the ground with your legs bent and your hands held lightly at the side of your head. Slowly curl upwards into a sitting position, hold for a couple of seconds, and release back down. Repeat the exercise, keeping your legs bent throughout.

Press your lower back into the floor.

Your legs should be bent all the time.

If this position is uncomfortable, bring your feet in closer to your body.

The curl
You could start with this easier version of the sit-up. With your feet apart, curl your body up and reach for your knees with outstretched arms.

The jump squat
Sprinters and middle- and long-distance runners need very strong leg muscles. This exercise works in two ways. Squatting strengthens the muscles that run in your thighs – the hamstrings at the back and the quadriceps at the front – while jumping increases your stamina.

1 Start with your feet shoulder-width apart and place your hands on your hips. You should also finish in this position.

2 Bend your knees and push your body downwards. Keep your back straight and try not to lean forwards.

Keep your back straight.

Keep your head up and look straight ahead.

Your legs should be straight as you jump up.

Point your toes downwards.

3 Leap up into the air quickly. Try to go as high as you can.

Repetitions
As you become stronger, increase the number of times you repeat each exercise.

Using a medicine ball

A medicine ball is a weighted leather or rubber ball. When you do exercises that involve a medicine ball, the ball provides resistance for you to work against. This is one of the best ways of improving your strength and speed.

1 Sit on the floor and ask a friend or your coach to gently throw a medicine ball to you. Lean back slightly as you catch the ball and make sure you keep your stomach pulled in.

Bring the ball into your chest as you catch it.

Keep pulling in your stomach.

2 Throw the medicine ball back to your partner. Use both hands and push your arms away from your chest. Rest for a couple of seconds and then repeat the exercise. Make sure you aim the ball accurately to avoid accidents.

Straighten your arms as you return the ball.

Raise your body into a sitting position.

Try to keep your feet on the ground.

Keep your legs bent.

Hamstring flicks

Try to make sure that you flick your legs at just the right moment during this exercise, otherwise your hamstrings will not benefit properly from the move.

1 Lie on the floor and ask a friend to roll a medicine ball down your back and your legs.

2 When the ball touches your heels, flick it upwards to your partner.

Flick the ball with your heels.

Make sure you roll the ball carefully.

Kick-outs

1 Lie on the floor with your arms by your side. Raise your legs off the ground and ask a friend to throw a ball at your feet.

Straighten your legs.

Support your weight with your arms.

2 With the soles of your feet together, kick the ball back to your partner.

Bring your knees in to your chest when you kick the ball.

Press your back into the ground.

Fun run

As their name suggests, fun runs are non-competitive races that are often held to benefit charities. Because they are not officially classed as races, there are no restrictions on age or distance, and participants range from experienced athletes using the race to improve their technique and stamina, to complete beginners running to raise funds for charity.

Hill running

This is an excellent way of strengthening your leg muscles and improving your stamina. Shorten your stride and practise running quickly up short hills or slowly up longer hills.

Cross-country

Include cross-country races in your winter training programme. These are usually run over about 5 km (3.2 miles), and often involve obstacles such as hills, streams, gates, and thick mud. The cross-country is excellent for building strength and stamina.

Race walking

Race walkers adapt the way they walk by rotating their hips to produce a faster, longer stride, right. Their feet must make continuous, unbroken contact with the ground, or they may be disqualified. Training works on improving the range of movement in the hips, as in hurdles (see pages 18–19).

The relay

ONE OF THE MOST EXCITING athletic events is the relay. It is often the highlight of major competitions such as the Olympics and is usually the last event to be held. Unlike most athletic events, the relay is a team event, in which four runners each run a section, called a leg, of the total distance. Each team member is picked for a particular strength. The fastest runner runs first, the strongest runners run second and last, and the best bend runner runs third. A tube called a baton is passed from the first runner to the second, and so on. The main relay events are the 4 x 100 m and the 4 x 400 m.

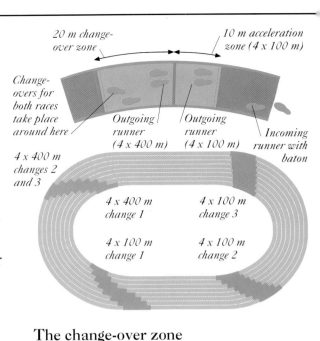

20 m change-over zone

10 m acceleration zone (4 x 100 m)

Change-overs for both races take place around here

Outgoing runner (4 x 400 m)

Outgoing runner (4 x 100 m)

Incoming runner with baton

4 x 400 m changes 2 and 3

4 x 400 m change 1

4 x 100 m change 3

4 x 100 m change 1

4 x 100 m change 2

The baton

A relay baton is a smooth, hollow tube about 30 cm (12 in) long and 12 cm (5 in) around. It can be made of wood, metal, or plastic and weighs only 50 grams (about 2 oz). The batons are usually brightly coloured to make them easier to see.

The change-over zone

The baton change-over must take place within a specific 20 m area, called the change-over zone. In the 4 x 100 m relay, this area is marked on the track in yellow; in the 4 x 400 m, it is marked in blue. If the change-over does not occur within this specified area, the team will be disqualified.

The change-over

A good change-over can save valuable seconds in a race. During training, practise handing over the baton to the team mate you will be running with. In both relays, the change-over should take place in the last 10 m of the zone, when both runners are running at the same speed. In the 4 x 100 m, the outgoing runner does not look back to receive the baton, but in the 4 x 400 m, which is very tiring, the outgoing runner looks back when the baton is passed.

Team work

I am the incoming runner in this race and am using the downsweep pass (see above right) to pass the baton to my team mate, Linford Christie.

The runners in this sequence are using the upsweep pass (see page 17).

1 As you sprint into the change-over zone, call out "hand" or "stick" to your team mate, who then stretches back her hand to receive the baton.

Bring the baton upwards.

Keep pumping this arm backwards and forwards.

As the incoming runner, it is your responsibility to make sure that the baton is passed safely.

The upsweep pass

Of the two relay passes, the upsweep pass is easier to learn and safer to use. The outgoing runner holds her arm low, which makes it easier for the incoming runner to place the baton in her hand.

1 When she hears a shout from the incoming runner, the outgoing runner stretches out her right hand, palm downwards. Her thumb and index finger should form a "V" shape.

Fingers and thumb form a "V" shape.

2 The incoming runner brings the baton up into the "V" of the outgoing runner's hand. Runner 1 should hold the first quarter of the baton, runner 2 the second quarter, and so on.

The runners' hands are very close in this pass.

3 The incoming runner lets go of the baton when she sees that the outgoing runner has grasped it. The baton is carried in the outgoing runner's right hand, and transferred to the next runner's left hand.

2 You should now both be running at the same speed. Bring the baton upwards and place it into the "V" shape formed by your team mate's outstretched hand.

The downsweep pass

When it is done properly, the downsweep pass is the quicker of the two relay passes. However, it is a more difficult pass because the outgoing runner holds her arm higher to receive the baton.

1 The incoming runner grips the end of the baton, while the outgoing runner pushes her right hand back, palm upwards.

Your palm should face upwards.

2 The incoming runner passes the baton downwards into the outstretched palm. The outgoing runner should form a "V" shape with her fingers and thumb.

Bring the baton downwards.   *Keep your fingers together.*

3 The outgoing runner takes the baton in her right hand, ready to pass it into the next runner's left hand.

Make sure you grasp the baton firmly.

3 With the baton safely in her hand, your team mate sprints off. You can start to slow down, but should not leave your lane until all the other runners have passed by.

🏃 Planning tactics

In training, work out where the incoming runner should be when the outgoing runner starts to run. This point is called the check mark and you can mark it on the track.

Don't look back as you reach back to receive the baton.

Keep running at full speed until you have passed on the baton.

Keep the baton in your right hand, ready to pass it into the next runner's left hand.

If you drop the baton, you, not your team mate, must pick it up. You can leave your lane to do this.

Hurdles

I N THE 1896 OLYMPICS, the first hurdles race was run over a distance of 100 m. The hurdles used in these early races were actually sheep barriers, which were nailed to the track. The barriers were extremely heavy and could seriously injure an athlete who knocked one over. Today, the main hurdling events are the 100 m (for women), the 110 m (for men), and the 400 m (for both). Modern hurdles consist of a wooden bar supported by two adjustable metal stands. They are not fixed to the track, but must be weighted so that it takes a force of at least 3.6 kg (8 lb) to knock one over.

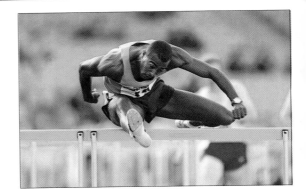

Looking ahead
As well as being physically demanding, hurdles also requires tremendous concentration. As you clear each hurdle, keep your head up and your eyes focused on the hurdle ahead, ready to sprint towards it.

Hurdle heights
The height of a hurdle varies according to the age and sex of the athletes in the race. Under 14 (U-14) boys and U-17 girls use the 76 cm (30 in) hurdle; U-15 boys, U-20 girls, and senior women use the 84 cm (34 in) hurdle; U-17 boys use the 91.4 cm (36 in) hurdle and senior men use the 106.7 cm (42 in) hurdle.

As you approach the hurdle, lift up your lead leg and bend your knee.

Drive forwards with your arms.

Lead leg

Straighten your lead leg so that your heel drives over the hurdle.

Use this arm for balance.

Try to turn your foot outwards to avoid knocking the hurdle over.

Trail leg

Drive yourself off the ground with your trail leg.

Bend your trail leg as your lead leg starts to cross the hurdle.

Hurdling technique
When you are hurdling, try to develop a smooth, continuous sprinting action that is only slightly interrupted when you jump over each hurdle. Work out the number of strides between the start of the race and the first hurdle so that you take off at the right spot with the correct leg (usually called the lead leg). This will help you to achieve a good hurdling rhythm, and will also help you to work out the number of strides to take between the rest of the hurdles.

Hurdles training

Like a sprinter (see pages 10/11), a hurdler needs to be fast and strong. However, hurdlers also need to work on increasing the range of movement in their hips and on their technique for clearing the hurdle. In this exercise, stand close to the side of a hurdle and ask a partner to support you as you practise bringing your trail leg over the hurdle.

Grip your partner's wrists for balance.

Your partner should bend his arms slightly as you come forwards.

Come forwards with your trail leg and drive your knee over the hurdle.

Point your toes outwards.

Keep your knee high, as if you were about to sprint off.

Watch your trail leg
This exercise is especially important because you can be disqualified if you let your leg trail around the outside of the hurdle.

Your trail leg should be about 60 cm (24 in) behind your lead leg.

Hamstring stretch

Try this additional stretch to further loosen your hamstrings – the main muscles used in hurdling. Place your leg on top of a hurdle and bend forwards to bring your chest onto your knee.

Keep this knee slightly bent.

Hold onto your ankle as you lower your chest onto your knee.

Try to keep your body as upright as possible; this will help you to clear the hurdle.

Pull your right arm back.

As you land, pull your right arm back so that your trail leg is pulled over the hurdle.

Sprint away from the hurdle in an upright position.

As you clear the hurdle, pull your trail leg up sharply. Try to keep your heel close to your bottom.

Knocking over a hurdle
You will not be disqualified if you accidentally knock over a hurdle during a race, but it will throw you off balance and could slow you down.

Bring your lead leg back onto the track quickly because you lose speed while you are in the air.

Try to land on the ball of your foot.

Triple jump

THE TRIPLE JUMP is the one of the most complex and demanding of the jumping events. Its origins can be traced back as far as the ancient Greek Olympics, when there were no set rules and jumpers could use two hops and a jump or three steps and a jump. Even in the first modern Olympics, the winner, James Conolly, won with two hops and a jump. Today, the rules dictate that jumpers must take a "hop, step, and jump", while trying to cover the greatest possible distance. As a triple jumper, you need to be springy, with very strong legs. Rhythm is also important as you need to make the flight times of each stage as equal as possible, and should be able to sense the TAA–TAA–TAA timing when you land.

Groin stretch

This stretch helps to loosen some of the muscles that you use during the hop and step flights. Turn to the side and take a large step forwards with your right leg. Bend your knee, making sure that you keep it directly above your ankle. Extend your left leg with your heel off the ground and feel the stretch in your upper thigh and groin as you lower your hips towards the ground. Repeat using your other leg.

Keep your back leg straight.

Don't let your knee go over your toes.

Keep your heel off the ground.

Hop, step ...

1 Try to build up your speed on the approach run to make up for the speed and distance you lose each time you take off. Limit the number of strides you take to your age. For example, if you are 11 years old, take 11 strides, if you are 12 take 12, and so on until you reach the age of 17.

During each stage of the triple jump, make sure that your trail leg does not touch the ground before the final landing or you will be disqualified.

Levels of effort
Try to distribute the amount of effort that you put into each phase as follows: 37% (hop) – 26% (step) – 37% (jump).

Pump your arms hard until you take off for the hop.

When you swing one arm forwards and one arm backwards, this swinging action is known as a single arm shift.

Bring your foot down and back slightly to maintain your speed. Try to hit the take-off board with a flat foot.

2 Your hop take off should be quick and "active". Strike the take-off board with a flat foot and drive your take-off leg forwards and upwards so that your thigh is parallel with the runway.

Bring your right leg back.

Swing your right knee forwards powerfully.

Extend this leg fully so that you take off at an angle of about 15–18°.

3 Swing your left leg through into a horizontal position so that it is parallel with the ground and drive your right knee back. Just as you are about to land, reach out with your left foot and "claw" the ground backwards to pull your body forwards.

Look straight ahead and keep your body upright.

Rest your hands on your thighs for balance.

This foot should be flat on the floor and pointing in the same direction as your body.

Inner thigh stretch

This stretch increases your flexibility, and can help you to avoid injury if you land awkwardly during one of the stages. With your legs apart, bend your right knee and feel the stretch in the inner thigh of your left leg as you lower your hips. Hold the position for a count of ten and then repeat on the other side.

Face forwards

Your foot should be directly below your knee and facing forwards.

Rest your hands lightly on the top of your thigh for balance.

Turn your foot forwards to increase the stretch.

Hold your head high to stop yourself tipping forwards.

4 When you land, your foot should be slightly ahead of your knees and hips. Your body is pulled forwards by the clawing action of your landing foot, and by swinging your right knee through.

Keep your body upright throughout each of the stages.

Bring your left leg through into a horizontal position.

Try to feel the TAA–TAA–TAA rhythm each time you land.

The angle of the step take off is about 13–15°, which is lower than the angle of the hop take off.

As you prepare to land, reach out with your left leg to "claw" the ground.

Try to keep your thigh parallel with the ground as your foot reaches out to land.

Swing your right knee through.

Try to land with a flat foot. Bend your knees as little as possible.

5 Still using a single arm swinging action, go into the step phase. The flight looks similar to that of the hop. With your legs wide apart, push your right leg upwards and drive it forwards.

Jump over on to the next page ...

Long jump

OF ALL THE JUMPING EVENTS, the long jump is perhaps the most natural to perform and the easiest to learn. The aim is to take off from behind a specific line and try to cover the longest distance possible before landing in a sand-filled pit. The event is made harder by the tremendous speeds that long jumpers have to reach in their approach run, as this directly affects the length of their jump. The most successful long jumpers are often built like sprinters – tall, with long legs and good explosive power. In training, they should also try to develop strength, a good sense of rhythm, and the ability to judge distances accurately.

Long jump

There are four distinct stages in the long jump: the approach run, the take-off, the flight, and the landing. You should hit the take-off board at maximum speed, so practise pacing your approach run to give the best possible start to your jump.

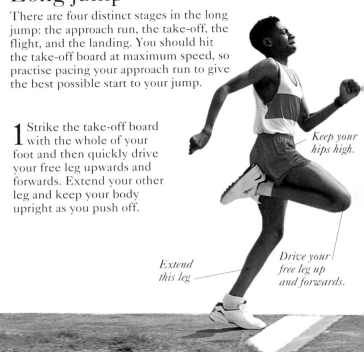

1 Strike the take-off board with the whole of your foot and then quickly drive your free leg upwards and forwards. Extend your other leg and keep your body upright as you push off.

Keep your hips high.

Extend this leg

Drive your free leg up and forwards.

... and jump

6 The step landing is the hardest of the three triple jump landings because it is done on your weakest leg and because you have lost a lot of your speed and momentum on the previous two take-offs. As you land, swing your arms forwards to prepare for your next take-off.

If you take off past the strip, your jump will be declared a "no jump".

Strip of modelling clay or damp sand.

Taking off

The wooden take-off board is about 20 cm (6 in) wide. It is embedded in the runway and is painted white so that it can be clearly seen. At the edge of the board is a strip of modelling clay or damp sand. If you make a mark in this strip, your jump will be a "no jump".

Bring your arms up together as you take off for the jump. This swinging action is a double arm shift.

Swing your free leg forwards to increase your momentum.

7 Drive off immediately with your landing leg. The jump take off is higher than those of the hop and the step, and has an angle of about 20–24°.

Move your arms at the same time as your legs.

Move your legs in a cycling action as you travel through the air.

3 As you prepare to land, bring your legs together and swing them out in front of your body. Keep your feet high and swing your arms back as your body comes forwards.

Swing your arms back.

Straighten your legs ahead of you.

Your approach run
As in triple jump, calculate the number of strides in your approach run according to your age.

4 Once your feet hit the sand, bend your knees slightly and try to pull yourself past the mark your feet have made.

Throw your arms forwards over your head.

Pull your body forwards so that you don't sit back in the sand.

Bend your knees as you land.

2 During the flight, try to take one or two strides with your legs. This action is called the hitch kick and it helps to propel your body forwards through the air.

8 As you bring your right knee through to meet your left knee, you appear to hang in the air momentarily until you fold your body forwards, ready to land. This movement is known as a "hang jump".

Measuring distances
Both the triple jump and the long jump are measured from the take-off board to the nearest mark in the sand. You should therefore always try to fall forwards when you land and walk out of the front of the pit. If you fall or walk backwards, your jump will be measured from that shorter distance.

Swing your arms and body forwards to stop yourself falling back when you straighten your legs.

Straighten your legs as you fold your body.

Keep your feet high so that they stay clear of the sand.

Bring your arms forwards and down towards the ground; this will pull your body over your feet.

Let your knees bend as you land; this will propel your body forwards past your footprints in the sand.

9 As you hit the sand, throw your arms forwards and let your knees bend slightly. This will stop your body from falling backwards when you land (see above).

High jump

ONE OF THE MOST important factors in the high jump is the equipment that the athletes have to land on. Up until the early 1960s, high jumpers had to land on sand, and were therefore forced to use a jumping technique which guaranteed a safe landing. The introduction of foam landing areas enabled athletes to concentrate on clearing the bar. Like the long and triple jumps, the high jump has four stages: the approach run, the take-off, clearing the bar, and landing.

Hold your legs below the knees and pull them into your chest.

Pull your chin up to your chest.

Feel the stretch in your spine as you curl up.

The curl
The Fosbury flop technique puts a lot of strain and pressure on your back. This exercise stretches the muscles in your back, and helps to prevent injuries while you are jumping. Lie flat on the floor and pull your knees in to your chest so that your body curls upwards.

The Fosbury flop
The two main types of high jump are the Fosbury flop and the scissors (see page 25). The flop was first used by the American athlete Dick Fosbury at the 1968 Olympics in Mexico. Instead of performing the usual straddle or scissors jump, Fosbury stunned the crowd by "flopping" over the bar backwards and landing on his back. Although this technique is slightly harder to learn than the scissors jump, it does allow you to jump much higher.

3 Your take-off foot should now be pointing in the direction in which you want to go. Keep your inside leg bent as you thrust your thigh upwards and forwards.

The run up for the Fosbury flop is "J"-shaped; straight at the beginning and slightly curved at the end.

1 Your approach run should consist of about 8–10 strides. The first 4–5 strides are straight, and allow you to build up speed, while the second 4–5 are curved to bring you up to the bar.

2 As you approach the bar, make your last strides shorter and quicker. Try to land on your heels, as this will allow you to lower your hips and bend your take-off leg, ready to jump.

Raise this arm as you take off.

Keep the shoulder nearest to the bar as high as possible.

Keep your inside leg bent.

Lean away from the bar on your approach run.

Bend your take-off leg as you prepare to jump.

Point your toes in the direction that you are jumping.

Scoring
You are allowed to attempt each jump three times. However, you will be disqualified after three consecutive failures, even if they are at different heights.

Back arch

For this exercise, in which you loosen up the muscles in your back, lie on the floor and place your hands under your shoulders. Keep your hips on the ground and push up slowly with your arms until your upper body is in an upright position. Hold the stretch for a count of ten, lower your body back to the starting position and then repeat.

Don't let your head tilt back.

Raise your body into an upright position.

Try to keep your hips on the ground and bend from your waist.

Keep your toes tucked under.

Try not to lock your elbows as you straighten your arms.

This picture shows a bent leg scissors jump.

Swing your inside leg upwards and over the bar. Your body should be in a sitting position.

Take off from your outside foot.

The scissors jump

Before the introduction of a foam landing area, the scissors jump was the only high jump technique that guaranteed a safe landing in the sand pit. The scissors jump is also the one that many beginners learn first because it helps them to develop a good take-off technique.

Jump upwards, rather than towards the bar.

4 As a result of the curved approach run, your body turns as you jump, and is propelled head first over the bar.

Pull your legs clear of the bar.

Aim to jump over the middle of the bar, which is the lowest part.

5 As you clear the bar, lift your head and shoulders to look at your feet. Keep your back straight and press your shoulders back and your heels in. This will prevent your hips from dropping and lift your legs up over the bar. Try to land on your back and shoulders.

Discus

THE DISCUS DATES BACK to the 8th century BC. The ancient Greek poet Homer makes several references to it throughout his work, and the famous bronze statue by the sculptor Myron (480–440 BC), the "*Discobolos*", depicts a discus thrower. The event involves an athlete rotating around a circle before releasing a flat, disc-like object called a discus. Up until 1912, the discus was thrown from an angled platform. Today, athletes have to throw from within a circle 2.5 m (8.2 ft) in diameter. They must make one and a half turns of the circle before they release the discus. This means that the action is more of a slinging one than a throw.

Straighten your back arm as you swing to stretch your shoulder and chest muscles.

Look over your shoulder at your outstretched arm.

Keep your hips facing fowards throughout.

Bend your knees slightly.

Loosening up
Prepare for the twisting, swinging action of the discus with this exercise. Stand with your feet hip-width apart and swing your arms from side to side. Twist from your waist and try to keep your hips facing forwards as you swing.

Rest the edge of the discus on the inside of your wrist.

Spread your fingers out evenly and tuck the tips under the discus.

The equipment
The discus is made of wood and is surrounded by a metal rim. The centre piece can be made from wood, metal, or rubber.

Safety
Because the discus is released after a turn, the throw must take place from inside a "cage" to avoid accidents.

The grip
Hold the discus loosely in the palm of your throwing hand with the rim resting on your fingertips. Your fingers can be spread out evenly (right), or you can keep your first two fingers together (left). In both grips, use your thumb to keep the discus firmly in position.

The palm of your hand should face downwards.

The standing throw
One of the best ways of learning how to throw the discus is to begin with a standing start. This will teach you the basics of the event and will also help with your future training. Using this technique, gradually build up your speed by swinging your arms and your body from your hips.

Pull your body and shoulder through by swinging your hips.

1 Stand with your feet hip-width apart and hold the discus in whichever hand feels most comfortable. Turn your body slightly as you extend your arm backwards.

Hands and feet

The feet positions shown here are for a right-handed thrower. If you are left-handed, use the opposite feet.

Start with your weight on your right foot.

2 Swing the discus forwards, turning your body forwards as you do so. Bring your opposite hand up to meet the discus during these practice throws if you are worried about dropping it.

The turn

Once you have mastered the swinging action, try turning as you throw. Start from the back of the circle and stand with your legs bent and slightly apart, and your arms wide.

Shift your weight onto the foot opposite your throwing arm and pivot around on this foot. Swing your body round and land on your other foot.

As you turn to the back of the circle for the second time, start to straighten your body and bring your throwing arm forwards in a wide, swinging action.

Release the discus and bring your right arm straight across your body and your right foot forwards to stop you falling over.

Briefly support the discus at the top of your swing, before bringing it back down for the next swing.

Try to swing your shoulder and your throwing arm slightly farther with each rotation.

Bend your knees slightly lower with your next swing.

With your weight on your right leg, pivot on your left foot.

Transfer your weight onto your left foot and lift your right heel off the ground.

3 Bring the discus up to the top of your swing. Your weight should now be on your left foot. Turn this foot to face the direction of your throw. This is the position you should be in just before you release the discus.

4 Go back to your starting position and repeat the sequence. Bend your knees as you rotate your body and gradually build up your speed and momentum.

1 Start with your feet apart, facing 12 o'clock.

2 Swing your right foot round to face 6 o'clock.

3 Bring your left foot round to face 6 o'clock.

4 With both feet facing 6 o'clock, you are ready to throw.

The release

Al Oerter, the American Olympic gold medallist, is seen here releasing the discus. He presses down on the leading edge of the discus so that it flies off at the correct angle.

Leaving the circle

Once you have completed your throw, make sure that you leave the turning circle from the back, or you will be disqualified.

Foot positions

The position of your feet when throwing the discus is crucial. In the diagram above, the circle has been divided up like a clock face to make the instructions easier to understand.

The follow-through

As the discus flies off Oerter's index finger, he steps forwards onto his right foot and lifts his left foot off the ground. This helps him to keep his balance and stay within the throwing circle.

Javelin

UNLIKE THE OTHER throwing events, the javelin takes place from a runway, rather than from within a throwing circle. The event has developed from the spears thrown by our ancestors during hunting and warfare, but the distances thrown today are far greater than they could ever have imagined. This is the result of improvements in javelin design and technique. In fact, in 1984 the javelin had to be redesigned because it was actually flying over the infield and onto the track – a distance of over 100 m (330 ft)!

The grip

The two main javelin grips are shown right. The middle finger grip (top), in which you grip the javelin with your middle finger and thumb, is the more natural of the two grips. In the "V" grip (bottom), the javelin rests between your first two fingers. This makes it easier to grip, but is often uncomfortable.

Middle finger grip

"V" grip

Cord grip

1 Try to build up speed on your approach run. Hold the javelin high with your palm facing upwards. This will help you to achieve the best result and avoid injury.

2 In the last strides of your approach run, stretch your throwing arm back so that the javelin is behind you. You should also drive your right knee high up into your last stride. This is called a cross-over stride.

The equipment
The javelin has a wooden or metal shaft, with a pointed metal head and a cord hand grip.

Shaft   Head

Shot put

PUTTING THE WEIGHT, as the shot was first called, originated at the Scottish Highland Games, possibly around the 14th century. The weights used were large stones, which were too heavy to be thrown, but which could be pushed one-handed from the shoulder. Today, a heavy metal ball called a shot is used instead of a stone, but the technique remains the same.

Putting technique
In the "linear" or "O'Brien" technique, you lean out over the back of the circle and then move across it, pushing the shot outwards and upwards from your shoulder. With the rotational technique, you spin within the circle to build up momentum before releasing the shot.

Extend this arm to help you balance.

Keep your elbow high throughout the sequence.

The equipment
The shot is a solid brass or iron ball. Its weight varies from 3.25 kg for U13 girls to 7.26 kg for men and 4 kg for women.

1 Stand with your feet about 60 cm (24 in) apart. Tuck the shot under your chin, keeping the elbow of your putting arm high.

2 Bring your feet together as you skip or shuffle to your left.

Holding the shot
Rest the shot at the base of three of the fingers on your throwing, or putting, hand. Use your thumb and little finger to hold it steady. The shot should remain tucked under your chin until just before you release it and should not touch your palm at any time. Remember the rule that "all shot putters should have a clean palm and a dirty neck"!

This "moving throw" is an easier version of the "linear" or "O'Brien" technique.

3 As a result of the cross-over stride, you will land on your right foot, with your body leaning back and your hips pushed forwards. This position makes it easier for you to throw the javelin. Hold the javelin high and behind your body.

Scoring
The javelin must land point first for your throw to be valid. The throw will be measured from the first mark the javelin makes.

4 Drive your left leg forwards to complete your last stride, leaving your right arm and the javelin behind your body. Bend your right leg slightly to drive your hips forwards. This will give your body a slightly arched shape. Swing your left arm outwards to help you balance.

5 Whip your chest and shoulders forwards as you bring your throwing arm through to release the javelin. Make sure you keep your elbow high throughout the release. This makes the javelin go high above your shoulder and head, and helps to avoid injuries to your elbow joint.

6 After you have released the javelin, your right leg will continue to come forwards into your next stride. Bend your leg to slow you down and to stop you from going forwards over the scratch line. You must remain behind this line until your throw has been measured, or it will be declared invalid.

---

3 Place your weight on your right foot when you land and bring your left leg forwards. Bend your knees, ready to push the shot away from your shoulder.

4 Swing your right hip around to bring your body forwards. Push the shot out from under your chin.

Scoring
The shot must land within a clearly-marked, 40° sector for your throw to be valid.

Flick the shot off your fingertips.

5 Try to push the shot upwards and forwards from your chin as quickly as possible. The higher and faster you release the shot, the farther it will travel.

6 To follow through after the release, bring your right leg forwards and bend it to prevent yourself going over the wooden stopboard at the front of the circle.

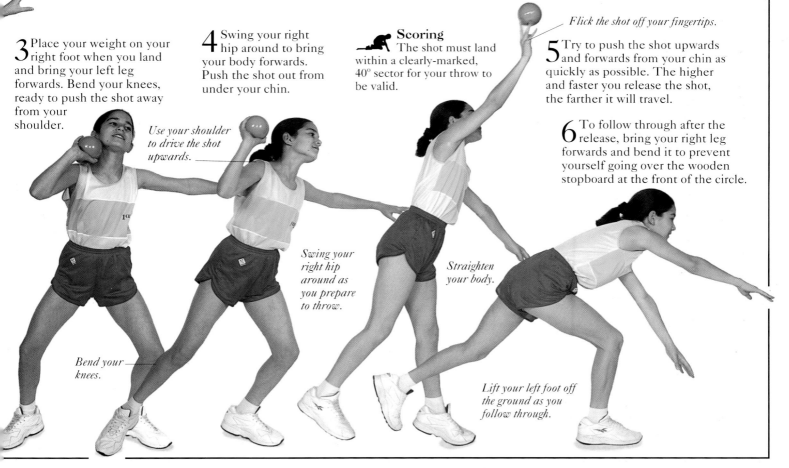

Use your shoulder to drive the shot upwards.

Swing your right hip around as you prepare to throw.

Straighten your body.

Bend your knees.

Lift your left foot off the ground as you follow through.

Combined events

THE DECATHLON and the heptathlon are designed to find the best all-round male and female athlete. The decathlon is for men and consists of 10 events. The first modern decathlon was held in Germany in 1911, and all the events took place on the same day. It appeared in the Olympics in 1912 and, like today's event, was held over two days. The heptathlon, which is for women and consists of seven events, is also held over two days. It was introduced in 1981 to replace the pentathlon, which had five events. The javelin and the 800 m were added, putting the emphasis on strength as well as speed. The winner in each combined event is decided by a scoring system, in which competitors win points for the time, distance, and speed achieved in each event. The athlete with the highest score wins.

Day one

The athlete shown in this sequence is Jackie Joyner Kersee of the United States, one of the top heptathletes.

1. 100 m hurdles
The events in the heptathlon and decathlon are carried out in the order shown here. There should be a 30 minute break between each event. The combined events test an athlete's speed, strength, agility, and endurance. Speed training for this first event – the 100 m hurdles – will also benefit the 200 m.

2. High jump
Technique and agility are put to the test in this second event, the high jump. The rules are the same as in the individual event, but the heptathletes are split up into groups of a similar standard. Athletes must ensure that they eat plenty of high-energy food throughout the day, and after the high jump is often a good opportunity to eat.

Day one

Daley Thompson of Great Britain, one of the greatest decathletes ever, is shown in this sequence.

1. 100 m
This is the first of the five events completed on day one. In the track events, the athletes are allowed three false starts, compared with the usual two.

2. Long jump
After the speed of the 100 m, the long jump tests the decathlete's technical ability. Combined event athletes must start each event, or they will be disqualified. However, if they fail to complete the event, for example, by missing a jump, they simply score no points in that event. This could be disastrous for their final score.

3. Shot put
As in the heptathlon, a large physique may be beneficial to this and the other throwing events, but could slow the decathlete down in the sprinting and 1500 m events.

4. High jump
Combined event athletes have to make the best use of their training time, and often train for similar events, such as the long jump, high jump, and the pole vault, at the same time.

5. 400 m
It is important to drink during the day, but particularly in hot climates and after a strenuous event such as the 400 m. This event is the final one of the first day, and the athletes can look forward to resting before the next day's events.

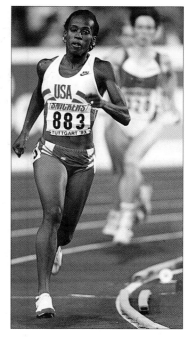

3. Shot put
This event tests an athlete's strength. The distances thrown in the heptathlon are often below those thrown in the individual events because the heptathlete is much lighter, and increasing her body weight for this event could ruin her performance in the other events. Athletes have only three attempts at the throwing events.

4. 200 m
This event comes at the end of the first day, when the athlete may be starting to feel tired. It is therefore a test of endurance as well as speed.

Day two

5. Long jump
Heptathletes have three attempts at the long jump, instead of the usual six. Speed is also vital in this event, to ensure a good approach run.

6. Javelin
Technical ability as well as upper body strength are vital to throwing the javelin. In the individual events, javelin throwers are small and light. Most heptathletes are similarly built and can often pick up a lot of points in this event.

7. 800 m
The key to this final event is endurance rather than speed. By this stage, the heptathlete should be concentrating on winning the points she needs to determine her final score, and should aim to pace herself.

Day two

6. 110 m hurdles
The scores on the second day are often lower as the athletes may be stiff and tired from the previous day. Day two begins with the challenging 110 m hurdles.

9. Javelin
By this stage of the competition, the decathlete will be feeling tired and must concentrate on throwing the javelin accurately to ensure points from this event. With his first "safe" throw, he should aim straight down the middle of the landing area. His second and third throws can then be used to improve the distance achieved.

7. Discus
The discus is often difficult because it requires perfect balance and coordination and the technique is much quicker than the other throwing events.

8. Pole vault
Pole vaulters need to be fast, strong, and supple to perform the complex series of movements involved in catapulting themselves over a bar using a fibreglass pole.

10. 1500 m
The most gruelling event of all, the 1500 m, is the last event. As with the women's 800 m, tactics are more important than speed.

Paralympic Games
Athletes with varying degrees of disabilities compete in the Paralympic Games. Like the Olympics, the Paralympics are held every four years, and wherever possible, they are staged in the same country as the Olympics. The first full Paralympic Games were held in Rome in 1960, and since 1976, the Winter Paralympics have also been held. Events include cycling and judo.

Index

Acknowledgments

Dorling Kindersley would like to thank the following people
for their help in the production of this book:

With special thanks to Rez Cameron for his technical input into the book and his expert advice at the photo sessions; all the Young Athletes for their patience and enthusiasm during the photography; Pat Fitzgerald and John Smith of Thames Valley Harriers for their help in organizing the venue and their support throughout this project; Sarah McClurey for invaluable additional advice on athletics; John Garrett and Paul Ryan for their professionalism and patience throughout the photography;

Chetan Joshi for design assistance; Floyd Sayers for organizing the kits.

Picture credits
B=bottom; L=left; R=right; C=centre; T=top. The publisher would like to thank the following for their kind permission to reproduce their photographs:
Action Plus/R. Francis 16cr, 31tcr; Tony Henshaw 31bl; Glyn Kirk back cover bl, 4cr, 4bc, 13c; **Agence Vandystadt**/ Laurent Zabulon 31tl; **Allsport**/Tony Duffy front

cover bl; Clive Mason front cover tl, 4bl, 15crb; G. Mortimore back cover br, 4tl, 31br; Mike Powell 30tc, 31tr; **Colorsport** 4cl, 11tr, 12t, 18tr, 27cr, 27br, 30bl, 30cl, 30bcl, 30cr, 30bcr, 31bl, 31bcl, 31br, 31bcr; **Mary Evans Picture Library** 5tl, 5ca; **John Hedgethorne** 15br; **Hulton Deutsch Collection** 5cr, 5cl; **Image Bank**/Leo Mason 31tcl; **Mark Shearman** 25tr; **Sporting Pictures** 4br, 5cb, 15bc, 30tr, 31cl.